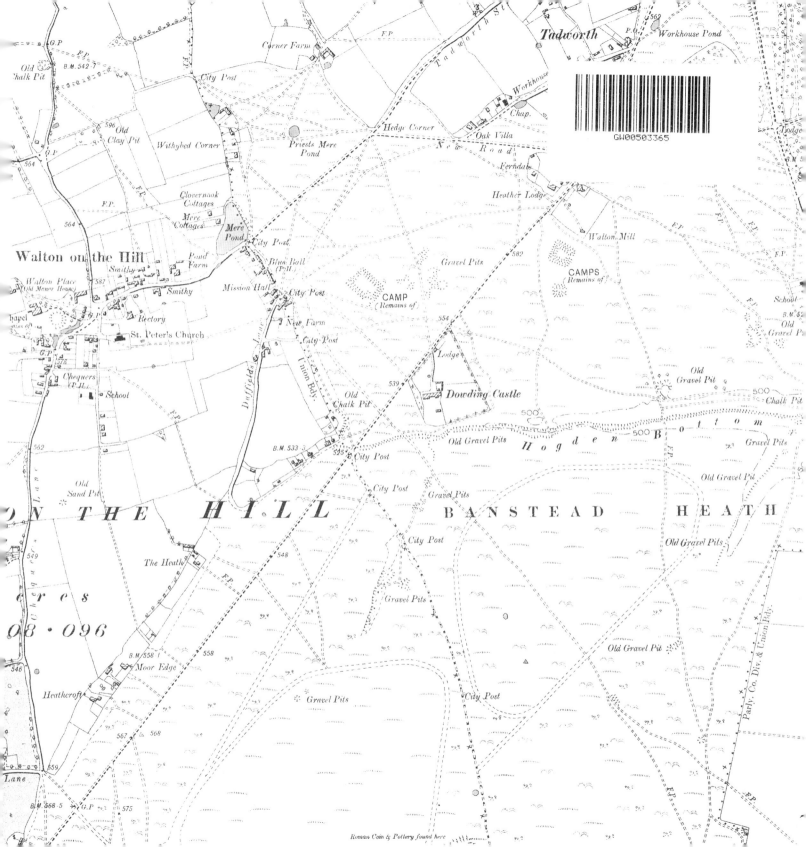

Tadworth

Workhouse Pond

Corner Farm

F.P.

City Post

Old Chalk Pit

B.M. 542·7

Withybed Corner

Hedge Corner

Oak Villa

New Road

Ferndale

596 Old Clay Pit

Priests Mere Pond

Heather Lodge

564

Clovernook Cottages

Walton Mill

582 CAMPS (Remains of)

G.P.

564

F.P.

Mere Cottages

Mere Pond

City Post

Gravel Pits

Walton on the Hill

Smithy

Pond Farm

Blue Ball (P.H.)

CAMP (Remains of)

Walton Place (Old Manor House)

587

Smithy

Mission Hall

City Post

554

School

Chapel

Rectory

New Farm

B.M. 5

St. Peter's Church

City Post

Lodge

Old Gravel Pit

G.P.

Duffields Lane

Union Bdy.

539

Dowding Castle

Old Gravel Pit

Chequers (P.H.)

School

Old Chalk Pit

525 City Post

500

500

Chalk Pit

562

B.M. 533·3

City Post

Hogden Bottom

Gravel Pits

Old Sand Pit

City Post

Old Gravel Pit

ON THE HILL

548

Gravel Pits

BANSTEAD HEATH

Old Gravel Pits

cres

The Heath

F.P.

08·096

549

Gravel Pits

546

B.M. 558·1

558

Moor Edge

Old Gravel Pit

Heathcroft

567 568

City Post

Parly. Co. Div. & Union Bdy.

559

Gravel Pits

Lane

B.M. 568·5 G.P. 575

Roman Coin & Pottery found here

WILD ABOUT
Walton & THE
Surrey Hills

TADWORTH, KINGSWOOD, EPSOM, LANGLEY VALE, DORKING & BOX HILL

By Andrew Wilson

Historical Consultants: The Walton & District Local History Society

In memory of my dear Mum and Dad, Ann and Martin Wilson,
and my two brothers Garnet and Nicholas,
all sadly gone but never ever forgotten

Kindly sponsored by

Clockwise from top left: The Horses down Ebbisham Lane, Mere Pond, Marbled White butterflies up on Box Hill and St Peter's Church.

Contents

Welcome to Wild about Walton & the Surrey Hills

Welcome to the latest edition in my series of village books. This particular one is perhaps my most personal to date in that it takes me back to where I was born; in part, a trip down memory lane but also a special tribute to those members of my family no longer with us.

What I particularly enjoy about compiling the photography for all my books is discovering wonderful places that I've never seen before. Langley Vale was one such place; tipped off by my brother who'd been there, what a delight it turned out to be. I even shared this with my daughter during the first lockdown, when we made a pilgrimage one evening in May to see the Regiment of Trees.

This year has not been the one we all expected or wanted and despite all that Covid could throw at us, I would like to thank all the people who have worked so tirelessly on my behalf to bring my books to life. I couldn't possibly mention everyone and I have made an effort to thank certain people within the relevant text. However, there are of course some stand out people, Jackie Godfrey and Robert Ruddell, who kindly provided all the background research and information to accompany all my pictures, including a scene setting history at the front. Emmeline Moore, from the Parish Magazine Window on Walton, who provided all the contacts and to one of those, Grant Webster, who runs the Walton Forum. Finally, Sue Edwards, who runs the local horticultural society, for introducing me to some of her members, some of whom appear in the book.

My books normally take upwards of 18 months to produce but what with Brexit and Covid, this particular book has taken me the best part of 3 years. They are expensive to produce and I am therefore extremely grateful to my sponsors for the help they are providing. I always try and work with local companies, who I feel have the most to gain from the association and this book is no exception. Firstly, Alan, Richard and Hamish from Michael Everett, the estate agents who literally cover the domain of the book, with branches in Banstead, Epsom and Walton of course. The same could be said for Downs, the solicitors, who cover much of this part of Surrey. Finally, there is KG Associates, the financial advisors and the preeminent St James Place Wealth Management practice in this part of North Surrey. Without their invaluable assistance I would not be able to do what I do, so do please think of them the next time you are in need of that kind of quality service.

I also started to work with a new designer on this book, Kieran Metcalfe from Ascent Creative, who came to me through a mutual love of photography. Thankfully, working on a book such as mine is what working online was invented for, so despite the pandemic, our new relationship worked out well.

I hope you enjoy my trip across the hills and dales of North Surrey and do drop us a line sometime and let me know what you liked the best?

Andrew Wilson, November 2020

To keep up to date with all the news about Walton, why not like the village's Facebook Page - *facebook.com/WaltonVillageForum*

Left: My springer spaniel, Josie, who despite her age was still able to join me from time to time, here pictured at the Golf Club and on the common. **Opposite**: an aerial view of Churchfield and the surrounding area dating from the 80s.

A History of the Area

by Jackie Godfrey

Excavations have indicated that there was some form of activity on Walton Heath during the Prehistoric and Iron Ages. Although neither are now visible, there are records of two Roman villas in the area, one on the Heath and the other in private gardens in Sandlands Road.

At the Norman Conquest the Manor was given to Richard de Tonbridge, passing through several owners before being acquired by the Crown. Henry VIII gave it to Catherine of Aragon as part of her marriage settlement, and then took it back again upon their divorce! There is a tradition that Anne of Cleves stayed there, but alas no hard evidence. In 1629 the Manor passed to the Carew family of Beddington and it remained in the family until 1864. They also owned the advowson, the right of appointment to a living from the church. Parts of the Manor House date back to the 14th century including the remnants of a hall and chapel but it remained a mere farmhouse until extensively remodelled in 1891. A mound or motte in the grounds suggests that it was a moot hill or meeting place although another view is that it may have been a Norman fortification.

The village was, to a large extent, self-governed by the Vestry, with churchwardens appointed by parishioners. There are records from 1700 showing the scope of duties and costs. Landowners were required to maintain drainage in order to keep roads in a good state of repair and ensure trees and hedges did not impede the carriageway. This was undertaken by the overseer's appointed surveyor. A petty constable was appointed and in 1828 was given a pair of pistols at a cost of £1.6s.0d. Rates were levied to pay the costs of such services.

The agricultural way of life meant some workers were in desperate straits through infirmity, old age or accidents and the village had a workhouse from 1797 to 1813. Schemes to manage the poor of parishes constantly exercised the government. A criticism was often voiced from those paying rates that relief from the local parish held down wages and promoted laziness.

A pair of local postcards (c1955)
© Heritage Photographic Resources / The Francis Frith Collection

Left: Riddell Memorial Hall - In 1909 the directors of Walton Heath Golf Club, including George Allardice Riddell, formed a Territorial Army Unit from their caddies and greens staff. They also subscribed for a Drill Hall with an indoor rifle range to be erected at the junction of Deans Lane and Meadow Walk. Throughout WWI a vast Army training camp covered much of the area between Epsom Downs, Tadworth and Walton and the building was used for entertaining their comrades and a few of the villagers. When Riddell died in 1934, his widow generously agreed to give it to the village. During WWII it was occupied by Foyles, the London booksellers, on payment of a weekly rental and an agreement that the villagers could use it on Saturdays for entertainment.

Below: Walton Oaks, Dorking Road - One of the 3 large houses that had previously occupied the Pfizer property (picture courtesy of Robert Ruddell).

Parishes were deemed responsible for the poor in their own parish and accounts dated 6 June 1825 include 'Gave widow Dean in illness 3s.6d', 'James Easers child, the father serving in the Militia 8s.0p'. Very occasionally, to avoid expenses to their own funds, an individual could be sent back to their own district at Walton's expense - £3.10s.0d was spent in May 1816 returning Elizabeth Harding to her own parish. The Vestry were also responsible, under a quota system, for recruiting and training a body of men that could be called on in times of emergency. Other tasks included arranging pauper funerals, bread and wine for services, payment to bell ringers, recording births, deaths and marriages, all of which fell to the church officials and was part of the Vestry duties.

The officials carrying out theseduties needed a place to meet, and records show they chose the Blue Ball and Chequers Inn. At one meeting, in 1847, it was agreed a stove was needed in the parish church but it seems that even though the church was heated, the meetings continued in local pubs and the Vestry remained as the village parliament until April 1895.

The church of St. Peter continued to play an important role in the administrative life of the village as well as leading the villagers in worship. A congregational church came in 1885, whilst Catholics were welcome to attend mass as Lady Killowen's private chapel at

Tadworth Court when she was in residence. On 25 January 1965 the foundation stone for a Catholic church, St John the Evangelist, was laid.

As a study for feudal villages Walton ticks many boxes; a church dating from 1268, perhaps older since it houses a lead font dated 1150-60, and a manor house part of which goes back to the 14th century. With a few significant houses, Walton was a fairly remote and contained village but two notable events gave impetus to its popularity and subsequent growth of the village - the arrival of rail transport in 1900 and the opening of Walton Heath golf course in 1904.

Construction of railway lines required vast swathes of land to be purchased and the remaining land was seen as a development and building opportunity. Walton became a sought-after area to live where influential members of the establishment, politicians, business men and the movers and shakers of the age could meet socially. The much-acclaimed golf course provided leisure for notable men such as statesmen David Lloyd George, who lived at Pinfold Manor, and also Winston Churchill.

A surge of house building began and continued until the outbreak of First World War. By 1922 the village was linked by a bus route from Morden underground station to Walton on the Hill and so, along with train, bus and motor vehicles the isolation of the village ended.

Retaining the spirit and community is now highly valued and whilst it is important to reflect on the turmoil and hardship of the past, it is good to appreciate and treasure our surrounding landscape and history.

By Jackie Godfrey,
The Walton and District Local History Society.

Walton's Local History Society was formed in 1990 with a view to preserving the historic buildings, records and antiquities of Walton on the Hill and surrounding parishes. It continues to arrange lectures on local history, produce newsletters and issue publications about the area.

For more information about the society and how to become a member please visit **waltonandtadworthlhs.org.uk**

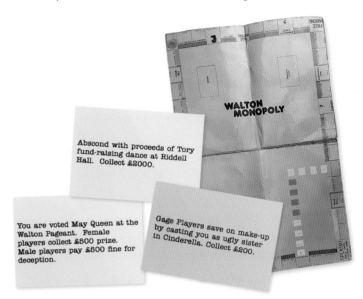

Above: A novelty version of the board game Monopoly featuring local places, which I played as a kid back in the 60's and early 70's. The game was put together by friends of my brother, Richard and Henry Macrory, and amazingly they still had it tucked away in the attic. I particularly liked some of the more irreverent Chance/ Community Chest cards. Interestingly, their mother, Lady Macrory, was the first president of the local history society, who have been so helpful in the putting together of this book.

Left: Mere Pond - The aerial images found in this book were kindly supplied by Surrey Visuals, a local company based in Walton in the Hill, who provide professional drone services.

The Walton Post Office, pictured in 1928 (top), and present-day (bottom)
Historical image © Heritage Photographic Resources / The Francis Frith Collection

Recollections from Walton in 1913 by a Mr Elliot and kindly leant to me by an old friend of my brothers, Richard Macrory, who like us used to live in Walton.

"On my way back from school, I was six at the time, we always had to call at the P.O. for our mail, no mail was delivered down at Wingfield Farm where I lived. There were no delivery motor vans in those days. The postmen either cycled or walked. Now we had a new Post Mistress who was Mrs Challis, sometimes she was helped out by one of her sons or daughters. During the 1914-18 war women helped out on the letters being delivered. Mrs J Taylor and my cousin, Mrs J Bennett were post women. They did the Walton on the Hill district. By the way, the post box or pillar box was positioned in the window of the shop" (and so it is if you look carefully at the picture above).

Mere Pond

One of the most delightful features of Walton is Mere Pond standing on the edge of the Heath. For many years an important source of water. In 1868 the Vestry, as the local council was known, concluded that it should be purified by a charcoal filter with a sunken pump. Paid for by public subscription it was in continuous use until 1898 when East Surrey Water Company provided a mains and storage water tower.

During the Second World War Canadian soldiers were billeted nearby and tested their jeeps and lorries prior to the Normandy invasion by driving them from one side of the pond to the other. They first water proofed them with wax and lifting the exhaust pipes higher in order to avoid them being submerged when driving off landing craft.

Over the last two years the village volunteers have worked to bring the pond back to life, dead fish have been removed, members of the golf club cleared fifty percent of the weed and the Epsom Fire Department helped to oxygenate the water.

Left: Mere Pond 1932
© Heritage Photographic Resources / The Francis Frith Collection
Right: Soldiers marching through Mere Pond 1942.
Reproduced with kind permission of the Walton and District Local History Society

Mere Pond - present day (top) and c1960 (bottom). Historical image © Heritage Photographic Resources / The Francis Frith Collection

Autumn and Winter

Mere Pond has always been a feature of the village for me ever since I dipped my fishing net here as a youngster in the early sixties. I walked over its surface during those freezing winters we used to gct, which we don't seem to have any more.

A small garden of remembrance was laid out on the bank alongside the pond and was formally opened by Dr Binney, Chairman of the local British Legion branch on Remembrance Day 1949. This commemorates the fallen of both the First World War 1914-18 and the Second World War 1939-1945 [South East Asia 1945-1946].

The Long Hot Summer

Even after a lot of rain during the winter of 2019/20, with lockdown being followed by two months of glorious weather it didn't take the pond long to dry out. The picture immediately right was taken in July 2020, and the other pictures were taken in the summer of 2018.

Picture overleaf:
The pond in April 2019.

St Peter's Church

There has been a church on this site since 1268. One of its oldest features is the 800 year old font which is constructed in lead and probably came from a small chapel which stood alongside the village's manor house. High in the tower are three bells; inscribed on the treble bell is "William Eldridge made mee 1681" and the tenor bell "Robertas: mot: me: facit: 1591".

In the church is the beautiful and intricate window installed in 1917 in memory of Captain Sydney Robert Sandeman who fell at St Julien, near Ypres, on the first day of the Second Battle of Ypres. The window is on the right hand side as you walk down the south aisle and was designed by Christopher Whitworth Whall. The well-known and admired stained glass artist lived in Dorking in the 19th century.

The Green

Historically the village green was common grassland with a pond where local inhabitants could water their cattle and other stock. Situated adjacent to the church and rectory, over the centuries Walton on the Hill's green became the focal gathering point for village folk.

Our four public houses

The Bell public house started life as a beer house and is situated at the very end of Withybed Corner and known in the village as 'The Rat'. The origin of its nickname is open to question. Some people believe it comes from the fact that the local stable lads brought pet rats to the pub.

A statutory 17th century listed building, the Fox and Hounds includes a flint outbuilding at the rear. Stag hunting used to be a popular sport and the huntsmen in their scarlet coats would meet with the hounds at The Fox and Hounds. The stag was let loose on the common and then hunted.

The oldest inn at Walton, the present building of the Blue Ball dates from Victorian times and was most likely erected during the 1880s, replacing a far older house whose history can be traced back to 1750 when it was known as the Chequer and later as the Crown. It has been refurbished on a number of occasions, the last time in 2015.

The Chequers inn can be traced back to 1814 though the present building dates from early in the 20th century. In 1903 a plan held by the brewers, Young & Co shows that there were more buildings on the site than at present and was then referred to as a public house, brew house and bakery. The Chequers remained a Free House until its sale to Young & Co in 1954.

Gun Corner

For some twenty years a 3-inch German field gun stood on the triangular island site at the junction of Walton Street and Ebbisham Lane. The gun was a trophy of the First World War and was given to the village to commemorate David Lloyd George's association with Walton. The gun stood on a concrete base in the centre of a well-kept garden planted with shrubs and bushes and enclosed with low posts and chains. With the outbreak of World War II the government commandeered all iron to help the war effort and the gun was sent for scrap.

THE GUN AND MANOR COTTAGE, WALTON-ON-THE-HILL.

Walton Street

Yeoman House (bottom picture) at 78 Walton Street is a 17th century listed house, formerly called the "Laurels". The house was once haunted by the ghost of a monk until it was exorcised.

The present blacksmith and farrier business has been in the family for over 70 years having been bought by James Arthur Ibbotson in 1944 from Bert Stillwell. Prior to that, there had been a farrier's business on the site for more than 150 years.

50th Anniversary May Pageant

Every year people come together to enjoy the annual May Pageant.

At the opening of the Tadworth Festival in 1949 Lord Simon spoke of the community spirit. "It is a part of good citizenship to take an interest in the community and to do our utmost to promote its happiness and progress ..... everyone who lives in the beautiful neighbourhood will be glad to do what he or she can do to foster the community spirit in our midst and make Tadworth one of the happiest and most contented areas in Surrey".

In 1951 the events lasted over a week and included sports meetings, a fete in the grounds of Chinthurst School, dances at both the village hall and the Lord Riddell Memorial Hall, cricket matches, athletics, a showing of the film *King Henry V*, culminating on Monday 16th July with the Chanticleer Puppets at Chinthurst School.

Having disappeared from the local calendar, the Walton Pageant was revived in 1969, on the common opposite The Blue Ball. My mother even had a stall back in the 80's (right), her sign courtesy of my wife and I (an all nighter I seem to remember, and before the time of the computer, in Letraset).

The Common

I played here a lot during my childhood and it is much changed since then, mainly with the growth of the trees.

Ebbisham Lane

Part of the pleasure of being a photographer is discovering new places and the countryside around Walton was one such delight. In particular, the farmland down Ebbisham Lane and the horses, especially these greys, which I met on several occasions.

Homes and Gardens

With many famous people being drawn to Walton between 1900 and 1930, there was a demand for fine properties and many prominent architects of the day were commissioned to design their homes. The two who made the most impact on the Edwardian character of the village were Percy Morley Horder whose buildings were increasingly Neo-Georgian fashion and Lawrence Stanley Crosbie, a Walton resident who designed the war memorial which stands in the churchyard of St. Peter the Apostle. Other notable architects included Sir Edwin Landseer Lutyens, Sir Edward Guy Dawber and Arthur C. Geen and several of their houses featured in the pages of Country Life between 1910 and 1912.

Many of these houses enjoyed a large garden but in recent years these have been built upon but some of the more notable ones remain. Together with the local horticultural society, we take a closer look at some of these over the following pages.

The Dormy House, a Sir Edwin Lutyen's creation with 16 bedrooms was built in 1906 to accommodate visitors to Walton Golf Club, and Gertrude Jekyll the notable gardener who collaborated with him on many of his houses, laid out the famous garden. In 1927 Lord Riddell solely owned it until his death in 1934 and during that period the house was known as Walton Heath House.

Opposite: *Walton Manor*

Walton Manor

The present manor house dates from 1891 but incorporates the walls of a stone-built manor of the 14th century. The part remaining consists of a two-storeyed great hall and a chapel. The old part of the building had been much altered since Jacobean times and by 1860 it had become a farmhouse. When William Rolle Malcolm bought the house in 1891 it was known in the village as "Walton Place". Rebuilt and extended by Richard Norman Shaw who specialised in country houses and also designed Scotland Yard, during the Second World War it was occupied by the Canadian Army and from 1967-1983 it was home to politician Lord Robens of Woldingham.

Thank you to the current owners (and Toast the dog) for kindly letting me in to take these pictures.

Nursery Road - Chussex

The foremost architect of his day Sir Edwin Landseer Lutyens built the house in 1908 for Herbert Fowler the architect who created the two magnificent courses on the Heath. Lutyens' first commission in Walton was Dormy House in Deans Lane built in 1906 to accommodate visitors to the Golf Club. He also designed an Orangery for The Island (originally known as Frogs Island) and Greenways in 1914 for Lady Londesborough.

Thank you to the current owners for inviting me in to their lovely home to take these pictures and for showing me some of the old sales brochures that they have (£9,750 - who would have believed that now?).

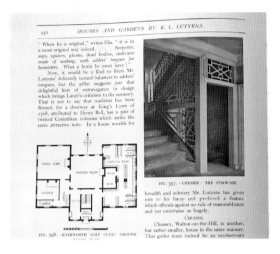

The present owners of Chussex discovered that over time the stairway had been moved to another part of the house; using photographs taken from an old edition of Country Life, they have carefully restored it to its original location and glory.

CHUSSEX - WALTON HEATH

Solicitors: Messrs. OSWALD HICKSON, COLLIER & CO.
Auctioneers: Messrs. KNIGHT, FRANK & RUTLEY

OUTSIDE is the stoke hole with independent furnaces or domestic hot water and central heating. Central Heating throughout. Company's Electric Light, Gas and Water, Telephone installed, Main drainage.

Conveniently situated to the house is an excellent Garage for 2 cars with independent heating arrangement. Other Outbuildings comprise—Potting shed, apple store, fruit house.

THE GARDENS AND GROUNDS, which have been carefully laid out and are well designed, lie to the south of the house and form an attractive feature. They include Rose garden with flagged walk and sundial, two lawns surrounded by yew hedges, grass Tennis Court, herbaceous borders, productive Kitchen garden, Fruit garden with forcing lights, the whole extending to about 2½ acres.

OUTGOINGS :—Tithe 10s 5d.   Land Tax Nil.

PRICE FREEHOLD   -   £9,750.

A CHAUFFEUR'S COTTAGE, a few minutes' walk from the house with 3 Bedrooms, Sitting room, Kitchen and Scullery is also for Sale
Price on application

Sole Agents :
KNIGHT, FRANK & RUTLEY
29 HANOVER SQUARE, W.1.
Telephone: MAYFAIR 3771 (10 Lines)   Telegrams: "GALLERIES · WESDO · LONDON"
Ref. No. 23555.

Church and Rectory
Walton on the Hill.

Nursery Road - Churchfield

Churchfield was where I was born back in 1956 and where I lived until my early twenties when I moved out. I was the youngest of 4 boys and it was the cue for my parents to consider downsizing, which in their case meant a smaller place that they designed for themselves literally at the bottom of the garden. The main house was spilt in two and remains that way to this day.

Built in 1913 for one of Lloyd George's minsters when he was Chancellor, the architect was Percy Morley Horder. One of the photographs is of me as a small kid with my brother Jeremy and our mother taken in the garden, probably around 1960. I love the old picture on the page opposite, when it was literally the field beside the church.

Nursery Road - Pinfold

Cliftondown (later Pinfold Manor) was David Lloyd George's home from 1913-19. He was Prime Minister for six years from 1916 and Walton's most notable resident. George Allardyce Riddell, his confidant, built the house for him and in February 1913 it was damaged by a bomb planted by the suffragettes, who are supposedly said to have gained access through this little window. The house enabled David to indulge in his two passions, golf and his secretary-mistress Frances Stevenson, who was thought to sometimes stay in our old house, Churchfield.

We used to find old telephone wires when playing in our garden and it was said that these were for the direct line that Lloyd George had to the house. Sounds a bit far fetched but we did used to find wires in the garden.

Nursery Road - Hurstwood

Hurstwood is directly next door to Churchfield and the current owners, Pat and Ana, were dear friends of my parents. The house, originally called Two Oaks, was built in 1925. Ana is very keen on her garden and something she is very proud of.

When my mother stopped driving and was finding it hard to get around, Ana would drive around and pick her up for tea (and the odd whisky) and then drive her back home again, now that's neighbourliness for you.

Deans Lane - The Merlins

The Merlins dates from 1904, with an extension in 1911. The current owners were again good friends of my parents and it was fun to meet with them when I visited to take these pictures and discover first-hand some of the great times they had with my parents.

Deans Lane - Redholm Corner

Deans Lane – Redholm Corner is part of the larger Redholm, which like Churchfield was designed by Percy Morley Horder and built in 1911. Now split into two, it must have been quite a place when it was all one.

The current owners are a charming couple and I had a great time photographing their fun garden, with its miniature cricketers and ducks.

Deans Lane - Redholm Cottage

Redholm Cottage was the gardener's cottage for Redholm, until it became a private dwelling in the 1950s and it was a pleasure to meet the current owner, who moved here with her late husband in 2003.

Deans Lane - Honeywood

Honeywood, compared to some of the others in this section, is far less grand, but still has a lovely garden. The owner is a proud member of the local horticultural society, about which more can be read on page 88, and regularly opens her garden up.

Number 2 Sandlands Road

Mereside or Number 2 Sandlands Road has a wonderful aspect, proudly sitting on the far side of the pond. Built in 1905 in Victorian style with arts and crafts influence, it was designed by a Mr Thompson, who is thought to be a protégé of the famous architect Sir Richard Norman Shaw. First occupants were the Warner family, with 9 children, who ran a grocery and drapery shop in the building now occupied by the Spaghetti Tree restaurant.

Thank you to David and Val for showing me around.

The End of the First Lockdown

The weekend of July 4th 2020 saw a further easing of the lockdown with pubs and restaurants opening and, for some, a well overdue haircut.

Walton Heath Golf Club

The arrival of the railway at Tadworth heralded the opening of Walton Heath Golf Club in 1904. Designed by Herbert Flower who was related by marriage to Sir Henry Cosmo Bonsor, chairman of South Eastern Railway, he transformed a wilderness and created the two wonderful championship courses we see today. The 18-hole Old Course was followed three years later by a 9-hole New Course, which by 1913 was extended by a further nine holes.

Walton Heath soon became a London club in the Surrey countryside with many members owning property in the village. On the eve of the First World War membership included the names of past (and future) prime ministers – Balfour, Bonar Law, Lloyd George and Winston Churchill – together with 24 Members of Parliament and 21 from the Upper House. The controversial George Allardyce Riddell, managing director of the News of the World, was a member from 1905 until his death in 1934. For many years he became a confidant of David Lloyd George and the club house often turned into a political annexe where state secrets were whispered through the cigar smoke.

In May 1935, Edward, Prince of Wales, was appointed its first Captain though his captaincy lasted longer than his reign as King Edward VIII and sadly the club never received a royal charter.

Uniquely the club has had only three professionals in the century since the club was incorporated in 1903. James Braid, who won the Open Championship five times, arrived at Walton Heath just a year later and remained a full-time club professional for 46 years, he was succeeded by Harry Busson, the legendary club maker who stayed for 27 years and finally Ken Macpherson who joined in 1977.

Over the years Walton Heath has hosted more than eighty significant amateur and professional championships, many of these historic challenge matches watched by crowds on the heath. From 1905-1969 the News of the World Match-Play Championships took place here, the Ryder Cup was played between the USA and Europe teams in 1981, there have been five European Opens and in 2018 Eddie Pepperell won the British Masters.

My father playing at Walton Heath in the 1980s

Walton Heath is one of the largest remaining areas of open heathland within the M25 and, unusually, a heath that lies on clay soil rather than sand. It is perhaps best known for its heather and come late summer it turns a beautiful purple and attracts numerous butterflies and other invertebrates. The heather is mainly the common variety of Calluna vulgaris often known as ling, together with dotted patches of bell heather, Erica cinerea.

With a profusion of heather strips running along the edge of the fairways, in summer when in flower it is an absolute delight to look at, but if a golfer does not hit straight along the fairways they can wave goodbye to the ball, lost forever in the thick and tangly bell heather.

Coal Posts

In Tadworth, Walton-on-the-Hill, or over Banstead and Walton heaths there is an abundance of white posts with an inscription: '24 & 25 VICT CAP 42'. They are the 'City posts' or 'Coal posts' and they mark the point at which duty became payable on coal coming into London - the revenue being used for a variety of public works. The posts were given Grade II listed status in 1985 and are listed monuments and they remind us of the times when those duties helped to rebuild St Paul's Cathedral and many other fine London buildings.

The British Masters 2018

What a lovely October day it turned out to be when I visited Walton Heath for the Masters Pro Am day in 2018 (unlike the competition for real, anyone can use a camera). Little did I know at the time that the professional player in the top middle picture, Shane Lowry, would go on to win The Open in 2019.

Besides Shane Lowry, the stars were really out in support of this event.

Left Top: Padraig Harrington is in the middle.
Middle: Tommy Fleetwood.
Bottom: Padraig was even happy to share a selfie with someone in the crowd.

Right top: Joining Shane were AP McCoy, Jenni Falconer and my wife's favourite, James Nesbitt.
Middle: Thomas Bjorn (our triumphant Ryder Cup captain) speaking to Lee Westwood.
Bottom: Dan Walker, Anton du Beke, Alexander Levy and Vernon Kay.

Opposite page top: James Nesbitt tees off.

Banstead Common

The Sportsman pub (pictured overleaf, bottom right), which some might never find, given it sits right in the common, at the end of Mogador Road, was reputedly the core of a building which had been the hunting lodge of King Henry VIII.

The Heasman were long term landlords of The Sportsman. Exercising the powers of the recently formed Banstead conservators, Harriet Heasman fell foul of Section C of Byelaw 6. In 1895 she was before the magistrates for abetting and procuring George Upfold who was probably an employee – he was referred to as her lad – for cutting and taking fern before the date prescribed by the conservators, the 10th Sept. It was stated she and her predecessor had for 27 years taken fern and had not received compensation for withdrawing her commoners' rights, therefore no wrong doing took place. It was ruled that the 1883 Act over-ruled such rights and Mrs Heasman was fined 2s 6d.

Commoners rights are traditional rights such as grazing and collecting gorse from land which is not owned by the individuals. Extinguishing such rights could be bought and this was necessary in the case of the construction of Banstead/Epsom railway line across common land.

The appeal of such payment lingered, more particularly among the less well off commoners. Those who no longer exercised their rights were keen to sell and subsequently there was less land on which to exercise commoner rights. Sir John William Cradock Hartopp recognised an opportunity to buy up land for development of housing, extraction of gravel and stripping off of turf.

Those who had retained commoners' rights were appalled as building began and the stripping of top soil commenced. They came together to oppose such action, through legal channels, supported by the Corporation of the City of London. In 1877 the Corporation took such steps as necessary for securing the preservation of Banstead Commons for the benefit of the people and contributed a large sum to the cause. The case which began in January 1877 was finally resolved in December 1889 in favour of the commoners. Further litigation continued until in June 1893 when The Metropolitan Commons (Banstead) Supplemental Act 1893 was confirmed which established a scheme for the local management and regulation of the Banstead Commons.

The Conservators first met on July 8th 1893 and Byelaws were drawn up.

A verse expressing the sentiments of the time:

They hang the man and flog the woman
Who steals the goose from off the common.
But let the greater criminal go loose
Who steals the common from the goose.

Clockwise from top left: Common Blue, Small Heath, Brown Argus and Meadow Brown.

Tadworth & Kingswood

Tadworth appears in the Domesday Book as Tadeorde and Tadorne. North Tadworth was given to William de Braiose and sublet to Halsart having 2 villagers and 5 smallholders whilst Odo, Bishop of Bayeux sublet South Tadworth to Radulf (Ralph) which consisted of 3 villagers, 4 smallholdings and 1 slave.

Dating back to the 18th century, Tadworth Court was owned in 1885 by Charles Arthur Russell, Baron Russell of Killowen, an Irish statesman and barrister who subsequently became Lord Chief Justice of England. The last owner was Charles Morton, a food manufacturer with factories in Cornwall, Aberdeen and on the Isle of Dogs and and a generous benefactor. Tadworth Court was purchased by Great Ormond Street Hospital in 1927 but by the early 80's was near collapse. A 'save our hospital' campaign started , which finally lead to a reprieve and new lease of life. Now a charity, The Children's Trust as it is known, Tadworth Court Children's Hospital has gone from strength to strength.

Sir Thomas Alcock, a Member of Parliament was keen to have a residence reflecting his status and by 1837 the Gothic mansion, Kingswood Warren had been built. On Sir Thomas' death the house was sold to Sir John Cradock Hartopp who subsequently went bankrupt; later it became the home of Sir Cosmo Bonsor, who was a major force behind bringing the railway to Kingswood.

By 1875 there was one school for Tadworth, Kingswood and Banstead and residents of Tadworth and Kingswood worshipped together at the church of Saint Andrew (pictured opposite). Today, Tadworth is regarded as a large suburban village.

Above left: *Tadworth Court as it is today from its lovely gardens. Right: As it was last century.*

Top: St John The Evangelist Church.
Bottom: The old station building, now a bar.

Facing Page:
Top Left and Right: Tadworth Station.
Bottom Left: Cross Road Shops.
Bottom Right: The Cricket Pitch.

Tadworth Station

The development of the villages of Tadworth and Walton on the Hill began following the construction of the Chipstead Valley Railway. The line from Purley to Kingswood was opened in 1897 and extended to Tadworth in July 1900. The single storey station was built over the line, on the north side of the Cross Road bridge, with a booking hall, waiting room, toilet facilities, bookstall and covered walkways leading to the platforms and other waiting rooms below. In 1905 an office building was erected for the estate agent Harrie Stacey on the west side of the station. The old station building has now become The Bridge restaurant.

Chinthurst School

Miss Alice Katherine Atkins founded Chinthurst in 1908 in a former perfume factory. Two years later the school was being run by the formidable Miss Thwaites and attended by thirty girls, some of them boarders between the ages of 8 and 15. A notable 11-year old pupil who attended in 1918 was Aileen Henderson who lived in The Grange at the junction of Heath Drive and Chequers Lane, she later became Lady Fox, the very distinguished and pioneering archaeologist. Chinthurst is now a leading co-educational school and part of the Reigate Grammar School family.

Kingswood, Walton & Tadworth Horticultural Society

The Horticultural Society of Kingswood, Walton and Tadworth was founded in 1904. Gardening is not a short-term game and this beautiful garden, The Firs (please also see the next page) has been developed for more than 40 years (here shown on their open day in April 2019). There is a continual battle, or perhaps balancing act, between nature and the gardener, currently the box caterpillar is a thorough nuisance.

The Society's shows have sections for baking, tea time treats such as Victoria sandwich, jams, preserves and chutney. Outings to visit other gardens remain popular and will, no doubt, be so again – they usually hold open days over a weekend in June, when several gardens are opened to the public across all three villages. A lovely aspect of the society is members visiting each other's gardens, cuttings and seeds are shared whilst enjoying tea.

The Firs &
The Pines

I paid a further visit to The Firs later in the summer of 2019 and the garden looked very different.

A huge thank you to Sue Edwards, who runs the local horticultural society, for all her help in introducing me to some of her members.

The Hoppety - Meare Close House

Formerly Proffits Farm, this Grade II listed house dates from the 1600's. I visited here as a child, as my mother used to bring me when she came to buy plants from Meare Close Nurseries, which was on the adjoining plot and closed in the 1990's. I particularly liked the pond and so was pleased to see that this was still very much a feature of the house; although I don't remember the abundance of marsh frogs that there are now. A lovely house and garden, it was put up for sale as we went to press.

Cross Road

The house was built in 1908 and the summerhouse, where I stood to admire the garden, has been a great refuge during lockdown, the owner tells me. The tower pictured at the front of the house, used to be where their son had his Lego train track. He's now 42 but the train track is still there apparently.

Tadworth Street

Built in 1904, the current owners took up residence in late 2009. They love the house, but both the house and garden needed a lot of work and over the last 11 years they have spent much of their time improving things.

More than anything, besides the satisfaction of living in a wonderful place it has also proved very therapeutic. They moved in following the sudden death of their 10 year old son, Joel, and the improvements to the house and garden gave them something to focus on.

2019, was the first year they had opened the garden for the public, and they took the opportunity to fundraise in their son's name for a child bereavement charity.

Chapel Road

The house was originally constructed as a two up two down c1690; the building situated between The Hoppety and Hunters Hall became known as Holly Cottage. Between the World Wars it operated as a laundry and ended the 20th Century incorporated into the garden centre, Meare Close Nurseries, that used to be here. It eventually fell into a state of disrepair and was purchased, sensitively extended and landscaped in 2004.

Kingswood

Archaeological finds in Lower Kingswood reveal that early Stone Age man was active in the area some 12,000 years ago. Kingswood is mentioned in the Domesday Book but strangely it appears to have been removed from the entry for the Manor of Ewell. Suspicion fell on Odo, the Bishop of Bayeux and William the Conqueror's half-brother who was a bit of a land-grabber. However, the tract of land was returned to the Crown and in the mid-12th century Henry II gave it to the Canons of Merton Priory. At the dissolution of the monasteries, Kingswood reverted back to the Crown and the wooded area became part of the Honour of Hampton Court, Henry VIII's vast hunting domain.

We have Cosmo Bonsor, chairman of the newly formed brewery company Watney Combe Reid to thank for being the prime mover behind the construction of the Chipstead Valley Railway which reached Kingswood in 1897 (see next page).

The building company of Richard Costain and Sons saw a business opportunity and by 1923 had purchased land in the area for residential development which also included a shopping parade to attract new residents. In 1925 Kingswood Tennis Club, top left, was established on a plot of land they specifically set aside for the purpose and two years later Kingswood Golf Club was built on the site of the former farm.

St Andrew's Church

Kingswood once had a chapel to serve the hamlet but nothing is known of it following the dissolution of the monasteries. In time Kingswood became part of the parish of Ewell and worshippers walked 5 miles to church – and 5 miles home again. Thomas Alcock from Kingswood Warren, along with other benefactors decided to build a small church with room for 152 worshippers. However, the congregation outgrew the church so Alcock, entirely at his own expense, built another one which was completed in 1852. The old church served as a parish hall until its demolition in the early twentieth century. Saint Andrew's lofty and distinctive steeple is visible for miles around.

Sally Lake and Gavin Temple married here on 26th June 2004. Sally's home was a stone's throw from the church.

Epsom & The Downs

Evacuations in 1938 unearthed a Bronze Age burial site at Epsom College whilst during the later Anglo-Saxon period remains of a settlement were discovered. The Domesday Book of 1086 states Epsom lay in the Copthorne Hundred consisting of around 44 households. The manor belonged to Chertsey Abbey until King Henry VIII's dissolution of monasteries between 1536 and 1541. By the 17th century it had developed into a small country town consisting of around 1086 households with agriculture, brewing and brickmaking providing the main employment.

Located where the permeable chalk of the North Downs meets the impermeable London clay, springs were discovered at Epsom, and one Henry Wicker is said to have discovered a well in 1611 from which the cattle refused to drink – it was found to contain magnesium sulphate, a purgative. After the Restoration of the monarchy in 1660, taking the waters became fashionable and it was visited by amongst others, King Charles II and Samuel Pepys. Being closer to London than Tunbridge Wells spa, it attracted the wealthy who built houses here; it is said that there are more late Stuart, Queen Anne and Georgian houses in Epsom than any other place in Surrey.

Picture courtesy of Surrey Visuals
www.surreyvisuals.co.uk

Epsom

The site of the clocktower was once the watch house where miscreants were locked up overnight before being escorted to a magistrate. In 1711 Celia Fiennes, the intrepid traveller, praised the clock that adorned that earlier building.

In 1847 a new clock tower was built. Henceforth all public events in Epsom involved the Clock Tower, processions passing by. Maybe the proudest moment was in September 1937 when the charter declaring that Epsom and Ewell had formed a Borough was handed over at the foot of the Tower.

Galileo

This fabulous new sculpture 'Evocation of Speed' by world-renowned equestrian artist, Judy Boyt, was commissioned to mark the millennium and was moved here to Market Square during 2020. It depicts Diomed, the winner of the first Derby and Galileo, the winner in 2001. A clever and stunning piece, you will notice on closer inspection that the jockey of the older horse is dressed in buttoned breeches and riding with long stirrups, while Galileo's jockey is in more modern racing silks and short stirrups. Since being named European Champion Three Year Old Colt in 2001, Galileo has gone on to become one of the most sought after sires in the world, siring a record 5 Derby winners.

The Ashley Centre

Mary Ashley, from whom the name derives and on whose property the centre sits on, lived in Ashley House until 1849. Mary is chiefly remembered as a benefactor to the local poor and much of the Ashley Centre was built on land that had at one time been her garden.

In 2007, after a change of ownership at the Centre, the new management decided to call it the Mall, but no-one else followed suit, so in 2009 it went back to being the Ashley Centre.

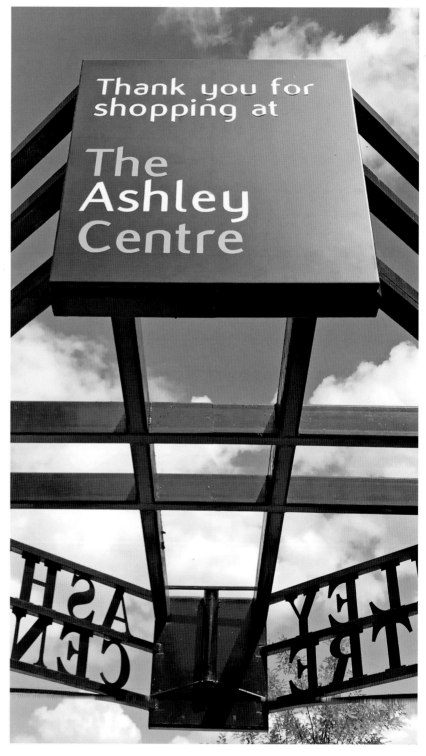

Thank you for shopping at

The Ashley Centre

Above: In the background is the original Clock House, Dorking Road, a Grade II listed building dating from the early 19th Century. The building in the foreground is the new home of one of our sponsors, KG Associates

The Derby Meeting - June 2019

At an Epsom May race meeting in 1779 Lord Derby established a one and a half mile race for three-year-old fillies which he named the Oaks, after a hunting lodge he owned on Epsom Downs. His filly won the race and at his post-race celebration, it was decided to hold another race for both colts and fillies the following year. Possible names for the race were discussed and the final two options were calling it the Derby, after himself, or the Bunbury after Sir Charles Bunbury, a member of the Jockey Club who was Derby's guest. According to legend the matter was settled in Derby's favour on the toss of a coin, although it seems likely that Bunbury deferred to his host.

The suffragette movement were certainly very busy in this area, as besides the attack on the Lloyd George's house (pages 50-52), perhaps more famously and sadly, at the 1913 Derby Emily Davison lost her life when she threw herself in front of the King's horse. Interestingly, it seems highly unlikely that Emily, without any form of commentary, would have known where in the running order the King's horse would have been. Also, from her position, standing low down on the bend, she was unlikely to have seen the first batch of runners coming until they were upon her. Ironically, the first horse she made contact with, was the King's horse and so doing brought her martyrdom the maximum publicity.

Epsom Common

Initially the common at Epsom stretched much further and the 600-acre site became known as Epsom Downs. It came under the control of the Lord of The Manor who only used the land for timber, hunting and fishing whilst commoners were allowed to collect firewood and graze their animals, mainly cattle and pigs. Under the ownership of the Abbey of Chertsey, monks in the 12th century created the Great Pond, stocking it with fish to provide food for the winter.

During 1618 a spring was discovered on the Common whose water contained magnesium sulphate – an aid for constipation – and so, for the next 100 years, Epsom was regarded as a spa town. Only a wishing well located in the middle of the Wells housing estate remains on the site of the spring and is a reminder of Epsom's most famous product, "Epsom Salts".

Epsom & Walton Downs is not common land and is now privately owned by Epsom Downs Racecourse with an Act of Parliament granting public access for "fresh air and exercise". However, the general public has a right of access on foot under the Epsom & Walton Downs Regulation Act 1984.

Langley Vale

One of the most enjoyable aspects of creating this book was being introduced to the work that the Woodland Trust have been doing at Langley Vale. On 25th June 2015, the 640 acres that make up Langley Vale Wood was officially named by the Princess Royal on behalf of the Woodland Trust, which has so far invested £1.2 million in a scheme to transform the area for nature.

Situated in the Epsom Downs area, Langley Vale is one of four woods across the UK planted by the Trust to commemorate the First World War. It contains more than 200,000 trees and sits between Woodcote Park Camp and Tadworth Camp where many thousands of new recruits were trained before being sent to fight on the front line.

The 'Regiment of Trees' (see pages 138-140) commemorates one particular morning in January 1915 when Lord Kitchener arrived with the French Minister of War to inspect the troops. The stone soldiers were installed in November 2019 and represent how the soldiers were lined up for inspection. Alongside them now are planted rows of whitebeam, beech, field maple and birch trees making up the 'Regiment of Trees'. The sculptures were commissioned by the Woodland Trust and created by artist and sculptor Patrick Walls. The stone is very hard-wearing sandstone from Hill House Edge Quarry on the edge of the Peak District. The artist wanted all the faces to be similar with few features, this was partly to give the soldiers a haunting presence but also to make them completely anonymous and to represent everyone so the viewer is able to impart their own interpretation and think of them as their own relative. The carving gets more detailed moving up the sculpture from the base to the head whilst the legs aren't defined, just roughed out with a punch chisel.

Amongst the Regiment of Trees can be found this plaque, celebrating the 3 millionth tree that the Woodland Trust have planted in collaboration with Sainsburys.

Commemorative Wreath

2018 was a big year for the Woodland Trust's project in Langley Vale and as part of the commemorations for the 100th anniversary for the ending of WW1, Victoria Westaway, a well-known willow and wire sculptor from Devon, was commissioned by the Trust to create a willow wreath installation as part of its Remembrance Trail.

Eleven logs were used to support the large willow wreath, with the Remembrance Exhortation printed on their ends (They shall grow not old, as we that are left grow old... We will remember them.) The eleven logs represent the 11th day of the 11th month and connect the willow wreath to the earth, giving it a sense of place and weight within Langley Vale Wood.

Victoria said at the time, 'she was moved by the process of weaving this piece of work, the many thousands of withies which were repeatedly woven into the sculpture and acted as a reminder of each individual who was involved in the conflict'. The opportunity to gather stories and memories of the public was the element that bought the piece to life.

The picture above was kindly supplied by Paul Taylor of *What's On In My Town Group* at the planting of 100 trees for the 100th anniversary of the end of World War 1 in 2018. *What's On In My Town Group* was founded in Epsom by Paul with the aim of bringing communities and businesses together as well as supporting local charities.

The Regiment of Trees

Clockwise from top left: Small Heath Butterfly, Roe Deer and Brimstone Butterflies. **Opposite**: Brown Argus

The Woodland Trust

The largest of four First World War Centenary Woods, Langley Vale Wood has pockets of ancient woodland, diverse and fascinating wildlife and flora, and stunning views over the rolling hills of the North Downs, as evidenced on the previous pages. The ambitious woodland creation scheme by the Woodland Trust has transformed the existing arable land into both a natural haven and a living memorial to those who sacrificed so much in the First World War, including a beautiful display of poppies each summer.

On one of my more recent visits I was pleased to bump into Keith Elliott, one of the many volunteers that help out and a local resident, Karl Tarratt, from the British Trust for Ornithology. They were catching young Stonechats in order to ring them. It was all very clever, as they were putting Karl's iPhone to good use and playing some Stonechat birdsong to attract others; it worked brilliantly, as these pictures demonstrate.

It was great to see first-hand the work being done here in order to encourage and preserve the local wildlife. They explained that earlier in the season they had put up an owl box and were amazed to discover that within six weeks, a pair of Barn Owls had taken up residence and successfully bred two chicks. Many thanks to Keith for these images.

Headley

The place name for Headley derives from the Anglo-Saxon word meaning a clearing overgrown with heather. Fragments of a coarse earthenware vessel dating back to Neolithic times were found near Toot Hill and by 1086 the Domesday Book tells us that Headley was a settlement consisting of twenty-two households. The first records of a church come after the Norman Conquest, the current parish church of St. Mary the Virgin was constructed in the 1850s using relatively local flint rubble.

Several estates grew up around the village, some with large houses. Headley House was owned by a member of the Ladbroke family, a distant cousin of James Weller Ladbroke who developed the Ladbroke estate in London's Notting Hill area in the mid nineteenth century. In 1895 the house was sold to Mr. Mappin, a London jeweller, but unfortunately the house was burned down before he could move in. A new house was built on the site and early in the Second World War was occupied by Joseph Kennedy, American Ambassador to Britain and father of future President John F. Kennedy. It was then taken over by the Canadian High Commission until the end of the war.

Headley Court started life as an Elizabethan farmhouse and rebuilt into an imposing mansion in 1899 by Walter Cunliffe, a member of the banking family who became chairman of the Bank of England. Used as the headquarters for the Canadian forces in Europe during World War II, it subsequently became an RAF and Joint Services rehabilitation centre until 2018. Another grand house is Headley Grove, a 19th century listed building which has been home to several famous people including the Maharaja of Baroda and comedian and actor Terry Thomas. During the 20th century more imposing residential houses were built including Tumber, Great Hayes and The Manor and Headley continues to be a favoured commuter village. The National Trust and Surrey Wildlife Trust control large areas, whilst former farmland has given way to riding establishments and horse pastures.

Picture courtesy of Surrey Visuals
www.surreyvisuals.co.uk

Much like Langley Vale, the open space around Headley has an abundance of flora and forna. From the cows, horses and foxes on the previous page, to the wonderful display of bluebells that can be found in the woods in the spring each year.

In the autumn if you look hard enough, you can also find the most wonderful fungi, which can even attract the odd slug photobomber! I like to call the ladybird image 'A lady caught in an Old Man's Beard'.

Headley Heath

Dorking

The Domesday Book notes that, with fifty six households, Dorking was among the larger settlements in the area. Its name comes from the Anglo-Saxon Dorchinges. Stane Street, which runs through the town, was a Roman road linking London and Chichester; initially built for military purposes, Roman settlements were established at stages along the route. The town's iconic symbol, the five-toed Dorking Chicken, is thought to have been brought to Britain by the Romans.

58 West Street Dorking was the home of William Mullins who set sail on the Mayflower in Sept 1620 with his wife and two of his children, along with servant Robert Carter. A shoemaker and businessman, he did not leave for religious reasons but took with him a large stock of boots and shoes. William, his wife, son and servant did not survive the first harsh winter but his daughter went on to marry and have ten children. It is claimed two American presidents, John Adams and John Quincy Adams are descendants.

Problems of transport over the chalk to the north and clay to the south impeded growth of the town until the coming of the Horsham to Epsom turnpike in 1755, the income from which was to improve and maintain roads. The area also attracted Londoners to Box Hill who appreciated the surrounding countryside and with the arrival of the railways more large houses were built in the town and by the late nineteenth century Dorking was surrounded by mansions sitting within extensive grounds.

Picture courtesy of Surrey Visuals
www.surreyvisuals.co.uk

St Martin's Church

The present church of St. Martin was originally built in the twelfth century, probably to replace an earlier one. Over the centuries it has been extended and, in 1877, a new tower and spire were added. The bells, which date back to 1626, were rehung in the new bell tower.

Prudential Cycle Race

Prudential RideLondon and Surrey Classic is a 100-mile route for amateur cyclists which takes place each year in August (not 2020 sadly). It was first held in 2011 acting as a test event for the Olympic cycling events to be held the following year. It starts and finishes on The Mall in London and features two laps of a 15.5 km circuit centred on Box Hill, with the professionals having to climb the notorious hill five times, pictured overleaf.

As we went to press it was sadly announced that this will be the last race as Surrey have declined to host it any more.

Denbies Wine Estate

The vineyard's name comes from John Denby who owned a farmhouse here in the 16th century. Jonathan Tyers, a dealer in furs and hides, acquired the house and turned it into a gentleman's residence. His wealth came from proprietorship of the Vauxhall Pleasure Gardens in London. After several changes of ownership it was sold to Thomas Cubitt who rebuilt it in the 1850s in a grand Italianate style. It is very much like Osborne House which he had designed for Queen Victoria and her husband on the Isle of Wight. The house at Denbies remained in the family and was requisitioned for use by the military in the Second World War. It was demolished when upkeep was deemed too expensive.

Now a family run business, Denbies Wine Estate comprises of over six hundred acres. The first vines which were planted in 1986 now cover more than 265 acres.

Denbies Hillside

With views towards Leith Hill, the highest point in south east England, Denbies Hillside is a great spot for wildlife-watching. The hillside is home to a great variety of plants and animals, including adonis blue and chalkhill blue (blue) butterflies.

IN LOVING CELEBRATION OF JOHN AND DIANA HARGREAVES

Leith Hill

The Gothic tower built on the summit of Leith Hill was erected by Richard Hull of nearby Leith Hill Place (opposite) in 1764. It consisted of two rooms, and the tower had a Latin inscription above the door announcing it had been built not only for his own pleasure but also for the enjoyment of others. When Hull died in 1772 at his request he was buried under the tower, the building was stripped of contents and it fell into ruin so the tower was filled with rubble and concrete thus blocking the entrance. In 1864 William John Evelyn decided to reopen it but the concrete made this difficult and so the turreted side-tower was added to allow access to the top of the tower.

Ralph Vaughan Williams and Leith Hill House

Josiah Wedgwood and his wife Caroline (née Darwin), grandparents of Ralph Vaughan Williams, bought Leith Hill Place in 1847 and his great uncle conducted many experiments in the grounds.

It was Ralph Vaughan Williams' home throughout his childhood until he left to go to Cambridge University. The panoramic views and surrounding beauty of the Surrey Hills and his affinity for the tranquillity of the area was a recurring theme throughout his life. He inherited the house from his brother and gave it to the National Trust in 1945.

Box Hill

With its mix of open woodland and chalk downland, Box Hill has a wealth of network walking trails which give wonderful views of the South Downs. It is named for the large number of box trees that grow here though no one is quite certain who planted them, or when. They are often attributed to Thomas Howard, 21st Earl of Arundel but they may date back to medieval times.

Norbury Park was a country house and estate near Mickleham. In 1848 Thomas Grissell, a railway engineer, bought the estate. It's no surprise then that he had a railway line built across his land. Grissell's grandson sold the estate to Leopold Salomans, a wealthy man who foresaw the potential growth of employers' liability insurance. The Box Hill estate was given to the nation by Leopold Salomon in 1914 and the memorial in his name was opened by his widow six years later. With its magnificent view overlooking Dorking it is one of the most popular viewpoints in the area.

© *Heritage Photographic Resources / The Francis Frith Collection*

Previous Page: Marbled White Butterflies. **This Page - Left:** Small Skipper. **Bottom Middle:** Small Heath. **Bottom Right:** Dark Green Fritillary.
Bottom opposite: A herd of Banded Galloway cows roam the hill throughout the year.

First Edition – © Unity Print and Publishing Limited 2020

Historical Consultants – Jackie Godfrey and Robert Ruddell The Walton and District Local History Society
www.waltonandtadworthlhs.org.uk

Proof reading – Caroline Macmillan –
www.westlondonwalks.co.uk

Designed by Ascent Creative
www.ascent-creative.co.uk

Printed by Page Brothers of Norwich
www.pagebros.co.uk

Bound by Green St Bindery of Oxford
www.maltbysbookbinders.co.uk

Colour management by Paul Sherfield of The Missing Horse Consultancy
www.missinghorsecons.co.uk

Published by Unity Print and Publishing Limited,
18 Dungarvan Avenue,
London SW15 5QU.

Tel: +44 (0)20 8487 2199
aw@unity-publishing.co.uk
www.wildlondon.co.uk

Andrew Wilson uses a Canon 6D with a variety of Canon lenses and an iPhone 11.

Prints are available from the images in this book, please contact Andrew for more information.

Follow Andrew on Twitter:
@wildlondonpics

Endpapers taken from an Ordnance Survey map dated 1897